PERMANENT STATE

PERMANENT STATE

Brian Henry

Threadsuns   2020
High Point, North Carolina

Published by Threadsuns, High Point, NC 27268

First Edition

24   23   22   21   20   5   4   3   2   1

ISBN   978-1-7346911-0-8

LIBRARY OF CONGRESS CONTROL NUMBER: 2020939835

Permanent State is set in Caslon, with Europa display.
Cover image taken from NASA.

Contents

Acknowledgments

Many thanks to Dara Wier and Factory Hollow Press for publishing some of these poems as the chapbook *Former Planet*, and to the editors of these magazines for first publishing various poems from the book, sometimes in different forms and under different titles:

1913
Apartment
Conjunctions
Connotation
The Homestead Review
The Laurel Review
Makeout Creek
New American Writing
Ocean State Review
The Offending Adam
Ping-Pong

Plume Poetry
Poetry International
Poets.org
RealPoetik
Talking River Review
This Corner
Tyger Burning
Virginia Quarterly Review
Volt
The Volta

Several poems also appeared (in English and in Slovenian translation) in the 2018 Vilenica International Literary Festival almanac and in *Megla, Oblaki, Blaženost in Tako Dalje* (*Fog, Clouds, Bliss, Etc.*), a bilingual chapbook published by Beletrina in 2018.

for Brynne and Beckett

WILDERNESS VERSION

I slipped inside
one person,
staggered out another.

WILD FIRE

in the next state down
thickens the air we're given.
The thick thick air.

WHOSE SILENCE

       Stopping to listen
and hearing nothing,

       hearing oneself
listening

       to a hum
one would call nothing,

       to a human
one would call nothing.

WHICH INFINITY

As one who
As one does

Scattered seeds
Aerated frown

As one who
As one does

Impossible figure
Aleph null

Good morning, asymptote
Good morning, wreck

WHAT EQUINOX

The day a throb,
this translation of mold
a new hell for the skull

(lens | temple | socket
—blur and ache and swell—
circumcised sight).

In the morning I traced
the line I'd have my tongue
take across your back.

In the evening my eyes find
—as you lean, back to me—
another, lower line.

The day shudders
into tomorrow's yawn,
that acrylic embrace.

But the day's no canvas
and I forgot
to mention the rain.

How it held the day
(all day)
in its parentheses.

WEST TELLURIDE

Untouched
by gravity,
your dream
cannot draw you down
or hold you under.
Your dream
cannot sink you.
This means, too,
it cannot buoy
or solace.
Cannot lift.
Inert, electric,
it just is
and then it isn't.

///

A blanket,
especially
when plural,
tends towards a heap.
Unless you do not
sleep.
Unless you are
ensconced
beneath, seeking
static by flipping
the fleece
covering you
away from you.

///

That speck
of dust,
its size,
is stuck
halfway
between Earth
and electron.
Every speck.

WEAK LUNGS

There, where
the breath stops
a breath too soon:

a space seeking air
to fill it
not filling.

TONGUE STRINGS

Slowly we still our own minor breath
until the lungs function
as one, for once.

THIS US

or the brunt
of what whittles us

are we atmosphere
shouldering our own climate
as if one sky

as if together
we shaped the sound
of what awaits us

breaks us
so we can put each other
back together

in the dark
no light to blind
or guide us

nothing to distract us
from us

THINGS' WILL

Where nothing'll
burn or even
split

by itself or
in twos

the air has
nothing here

no effect
here

the air is
all around here

things pay it no mind
will not combust
or divide

become any less
(become any
thing less)

what is there
to learn from this

THE TOWER

We arrived expecting edification
but found a building instead.
It reflected whatever stood
before it, plus the sky, and trees
if there were trees there to be reflected.
You said the clouds were like crowns
though they moved, and were white, not green.

Everything seemed darker outside—
clouds nearly black, human faces masked,
bodies columns of ash. Some passed
through the spinning door and into the interior—
a gilded heaven, we heard, every surface
a choir. The light in there, they said,
was flattering, hopeless, and without end.

SYLLABLE SOUNDING

This heritage   my powerline
my tobacco-born valley listing skyward
almost in unison   an integral undwelling

My heritage   this plagiarist
this speck of star on the page
a lash in my eye mottling it

A field of corn   I whisper
and you agree   for now
unsure of what the eye is streaming

but this wind   you feel it
and know it to be true
its touch   all that is falling

Smalltalk is dead   you killed it
so we follow the tracks
some minor vehicle laid here for us

as a welcome
and when we arrive we say welcome

STAGE MOTHER

in a stage whisper
claims to not know
you at all.

SPRING'S WINTER

Olfactory cilia thinned to nil,
unvarnished spirits, we smell
only what we kill to remove
via edge, muscle, and mineral.
The noisome mustard rubbed
down to brown, rubbed further
into nothing, then brought back
to a white that shows nothing,
covers all as if its point
as a color were covering,
the interior has not only changed,
it's shifted, these new vapors
dulling the senses, no longer
morose, stroked otiose as if
by happenstance, windows open,
almost, nevertheless the air
has scraped itself to a standstill,
like us, like the eyes that used to
rove and spin, shudder at the sight
or thought of the static,
the orchestrated, the mono-
chromatic: what loveliness
such swerving, if seen from this
angle, is. Another would sink
the entire enterprise, bring

the walls down with our screams,
the dog's versions of,
require one or both of us
to auscultate all four,
ear to glass to enpapered
gypsum plaster, our pinna
punctuating wall after wall
after wall. Of course, it all
depends, or at least rests,
on perspective and distance,
on how the overhead light
is doing, we've considered
changing it, from dead
fluorescence to halogen,
the better to burn our eyes out,
dear, a track of minor suns
pummeling us from our own
sorry ceiling. We take turns
making executive decisions,
can't remember who opted
for natural light, that is
to say, perpetual darkness
so as to usher in (postpone?)
the elections, forestall our
inauguration, ceremonies
of any stripe anathema within
these walls, which abide only
the shaky hands that we hold
out to each other in mutual
admiration, harnessed trust.
Given scraps or stripes, we pull

ourselves up, on level with
this design passed down to us
against our will, against
our better, harsher judgment.

SPRING THAW

No need for the usual
congeries of reasons
not to leave the house
(rain, chill, gray;
squirrel, grackle, sky)
if one wishes to remain
indoors.
             Inside, of course,
is where the action is.
Outside, nothing but mud
and neighbors staring out
windows, wondering how
privacy fences have kept them
from cudgeling each other
with whatever garden tools
are handy, left outside to rust
—no, out of carelessness
of mind and eye.
Then the sky gets wiped
and we wake to sun, mud, decay,
the ice in the culvert bound
to leave today, for sure,
and slip in sheets along the concrete
to the creek, conduit to a pond
half a mile away,
one grave to another.

SPRING CLEAN

Paint the walls Chantilly Lace.
Paint the trim White Wedding.
Black out the windows, spray tan the doors.
Turn on the box fan, scatter the spores.
Every particle here acts like a wave.
Dust mites cluster in the bedding.
Rip up the carpet, remove the padding.
Untack the tack strips, whiten your teeth.
Pop up the plywood, scry what's beneath.
Someone at some point used too much force.
Push further, past the joists and wires
until through what was a ceiling
you see a floor.

SOUTH INTERLARD

Here where
adolescence
and indecision
are paint colors,
we cycle:

rebeldom
then maelstrom,
a spotting scope
in a rifle case,
reveille then
defenestration.

A fortune told
a soft occupation.

Somehow we missed
our assassination.

SOBRIETY'S ITCH

Of course
there's a catch.

SO COME

These arms, after all,
are open for no one
else. Posture of air
if you stay where you are,
over there, farther
than far. Dim and low,
the strains filtering air
from where neither
of us can see or know.
If you must collapse,
fall into me upon
finding me, then do.

SMALL TALK

kills
a word
at a time.

SILENT FIELD

Slurred with
words.

SAINT SOUL

is caught between
train cars.
          In the vestibule
he is trapped,
on his way from one
to another,
but is, now,
between.
Everything is louder here,
thinks Saint Soul.
The door behind me has closed,
the door in front of me broken.
It will not open.
Everything is hotter here,
thinks Saint Soul,
and if it were winter,
it would be colder.
Where would I be, now,
if my motion
had been maintained—
in the quiet car,
          my head
in the lap of the angel
I saw board,
who boarded
under my watch
-ful and disfiguring gaze.

SAFEST HUMAN

woke choking   dying with some thing stuck
pointer down throat to fish the foreign out

rushed to the bathroom sink to rinse   take
the faucet's flawed offering   woke
into the attack so tight it crunched there

welcome weakness   welcome shock   pills
in one hand   pills in the other
no enchanted exit   no sure sure

when did you drive your head through the door
bits of hair and scalp now adorn

black eye for a bloody nose   broken arm
for a broken nose   concussion for a

the mouth when it yawned ripped open
the chin split down the middle by a tree

the phone torn from the wall   every picture
burned   she bleached herself to rid herself

the punch hurt no more than a punch
but the stone in the ring slit my arm   baby river

he was rolling on the asphalt with the other
when the other decided to bite   a part of him
in my pocket   later it reconnected

too much volume and my fist strikes my temple
strikes until the sound is no sound

as when a migraine is memory when
the head hits the wall   another pain

to drown   the aura   a concrete prayer
transporting oneself through the surface

seeing oneself to one side   a blur
that marks   is   every surface

my lie   he threw me against the ceiling
the truth   he threw me against the wall

the bruises on my back   the bruise in my skull
the feeling   for half a second   of flight

his hands around my neck   my back
against the fridge   his eyes squeezed to slits

no worse than the belt against my thighs
a few lashes in exchange   how loud those welts

woke seeing a figure beside the bed
destroyed the lamp   woke seeing a figure beside
the bed   hurled myself against the wall

woke seeing a figure beside the bed   leaped
to attack the iron upright on its board
woke seeing a figure beside the bed

woke choking   dying with some thing stuck
my spleen in my clotted throat

the boy swung in circles by his arms
this boy knocked from another's shoulders

that boy lifted and dropped   head
abounce on the grassless field

RIVER FIXTURE

You break your hold
ing pattern and your feet suck in

to the sludge of mud and leaves
slathering this speck of water,
stones dulled by the mixture,

rooting yourself there,
stiffening into fixture,
softened and softer, after.

But the shifting cold stirs
you and you step
forward as if to cross.

PUSH MOWER

The tangled bank
pulls, you
lean.

PREVENTIVE MEASURES

1.

Putt-Putt shuffles around the yard, mowing sticks, weeds, the pubic patches of grass wherever he'd scattered seeds. He stops at the far front corner of the house, where Grimace cannot see and where Grimace does not go. She darts from car to door, never strays from the concrete walk that divides one type of weed from another. Never ventures from the porch, to the side or back yard. A pine leans over the house. An oak drops limbs as long as the car. The pileated woodpecker perforates the masonite. Sometimes a pair of eyes appears at the window: a princess, locked inside.

2.

Putt-Putt shuffles around the yard, orange extension cord trailing, orange leaf blower in hand. He nudges the leaves into little piles, directs some toward the ditch. Gravity does the rest. He stops at the front corner of the house, where Grimace cannot see and where Grimace will not go. The princess sits on the porch, gnawing a popsicle. A large oak cradles a fallen limb. Grimace is inside trying to find her elbow. The princess goes inside. Putt-Putt draws a line of leaves along the side of the yard furthest from the driveway. The sun is setting, there are four small clumps of leaves, a ditch full of leaves, a strip of leaves on the property line. He scans the fruits of his labor, goes inside.

3.

A foot of snow overnight, the yellow house now part white. Putt-Putt shuffles around the house, gathering warmish clothing, princess in tow. Grimace is eating something with bones. The princess flaps in the front yard, face first, as if expelled from the assholes of angels. Putt-Putt peers at the property line, the snow having erased all difference at ground level. Upstairs, Grimace has wedged herself into the shower stall, vows not to come out until spring thaw. The sidewalk knows it will feel like the side and back yard: lonely, feral. Putt-Putt shuffles after the princess into the front door. Some snow falls onto the steps as the door limps shut.

PRESIDENTIAL WATER

Some scapegrace over-exerting himself, suffering around the yard. Worm, termite, beetle, worm. A clean hole—snake or spider. Soil moves easy, won't complain. The boy stomps it, a billion dwarf planets. A shooting star is not a star. Even if you could stay afloat on Jupiter, gravity would crush you. Caroline Harrison died in her office, her widower married her niece. Only the outer planets have rings.

///

Martha Dandridge Custis Washington took her time. No horse loves its rider. After the war, he tried to settle down. Anything divided by zero is infinity. Peggy Parish didn't die, she's in the land of Nod. Gerald Ford is resting in Michigan. A bee has bored its way into the deck—a clean hole. Whatever happened to the verdant green? Mercury has lost its moons.

///

If it splits, it's not a dinosaur bone. Violin, swivel chair, elevated bed. I was a feckless spendthrift. A million million is a trillion. Rachel Jackson died before Andy was elected. Saturn's rings shine (a clean hole). The palm was made to blister and moil. Row me out on the pond. Into that mosquito cloud.

///

The surface of Eris is sentient. And then there's the inner belt. Vegan mice eat vegan cheese. One tick at a time. Hannah Van Buren was no wastrel. A deer has scraped a clean hole by the begonias. Beneath the dirt, clay. Beneath the clay, bones. You cannot talk about fractions of animals.

///

Tuesday wants to be blue. Like Frances Cleveland. To lead a hugger-mugger life. Venus is just hanging up there. Elk litter the hill above the hot springs. The thermal panic grass immune to locusts. Multiplication, like addition, is commutative; multiplication, like addition, is associative. A swift yet firm tug should remove that tooth. A clean hole.

///

Uranus' rings go like this. Push outward toward less. A googol divided by ten is a dogillion. That is a neologism. George Washington was a biscuit. A clean hole. Open like petals after rain. A ladybird walks the curtain. Letitia Tyler would know how to dissuade it.

///

If I fall into a hole I'll see Ellen Arthur. A clean hole. Here is where you come up with a metaphor. The sister is a star she shines so bright. It's always better to be prime. A firefly disports in the yard. The boy swivels after it. Watch your step. Mars is rusty.

///

A clean hole. The dog revolves around the yard. Neptune saunters beyond beyond. To slake his desire for regular orbits. Here come the fire ants. Sarah Polk used grits to burst their bellies. Otherwise they breed factorial. Europe divided by Europe equals Europe error. There's no such thing as rain.

///

Dolly Madison serviced two Presidents. Three halves is improper. The girl scurries up the door jamb. The praying mantis rips a clean hole. Ne plus ultra of something or other. Earth grinds onward. The boy at the chalkboard, the dog under the table. The voice on the other end. We're strangers to strangers.

PISSING BLOOD

Synecdoche,
not metonymy.

PHANTOM CRYSTAL

with nothing
with
-in.

PERMANENT STATE

How did you get here? Why did you come?
Is the leaf-stripped oak strong enough
For the journey you've planned?
And what about your coat? I notice it's thin,
Worry you might shiver yourself right off
And no one would notice since you're already dead.
Sad then, your loss when it occurred.
Sadder now, the return.
No ghost should have to suffer again.
But we both know there is no place here for *should*s,
Only *is*es and *are*s and *was*es and *were*s.
There is no place here for promises, for dreams,
Those made of nothing, being nothing but words.

PERIODIC TABLE

Come morning, we spun out the door,
down the stairs and into the leaf-
sodden yard toward the street, wet
and covered in what the trees lost
overnight. They were still standing,
only small branches had fallen—
nothing to damage or distress.
Even yard signs remained, poking us
in the eye to remind us
we've never belonged here.
There are words on the signs, ciphers,
we tell each other, no more
than the badge on the back of that car.
But we are not speaking, no words
are being spoken here, on this
wet street barely mussed by the rain
and wind that leveled the coast east
of here. "Fortune" once came to mind,
quickly and without thought.
But it's been replaced by "grind,"
as in "The days grind us down,
into submission." To wake and nudge
oneself into something
like a day, something like alert-
ness, to prepare to face the world,
or not, to listen and prepare

for a storm that could burst
any time, for any (or no) reason,
to stagger like this until dark,
then rest and measure the pieces
of you the day has ground into
dead matter, not flakes of skin or
bits of nail, but pieces of you,
inside you, untouched, unexplained
by the known elements.

OPEN SOURCE

Sodden field,
broken span.

OKLAHOMA PURCHASE

William Howard Taft wouldn't drink before dark.
John Tyler fainted when he teetered off his horse.
Millard Fillmore never returned that silver dollar.
Woodrow Wilson broke down only in public.
Oatmeal nauseated Dwight Eisenhower.
The first man in space was Grover Cleveland.
James Monroe spent his dotage in a haberdashery.
The furthest Jimmy Carter could see
was into the eyes of James Madison.
Andrew Jackson invented the scratching post.
Warren Harding could square a circle.
George Washington loved his pony.
Herbert Hoover sanded his own table.
William Jefferson Clinton carried a heavy load
all the way to Grover Cleveland (the first, not his clone).
John Quincy Adams pulled the plug.
George Bush rocked himself to sleep.
Lyndon Johnson forgot a thing or two,
which much amused William Henry Harrison.
John F. Kennedy caulked a mean caulk line.
Thomas Jefferson could start a fire with his bare hands.
Andrew Johnson loved to hop over Martin Van Buren.
George W. Bush preferred a gibbous moon,
unlike Calvin Coolidge, who liked it new.
Theodore Roosevelt snored so loudly
he woke up Barack Obama.

The only friend of Franklin Pierce
was a forlorn Ronald Reagan.
Abraham Lincoln could carry a hog in each arm,
while Gerald Ford could barely lift a finger.
Benjamin Harrison never spanked his children,
nor did the otherwise stringent James Buchanan.
William McKinley refused to watch television.
James Knox Polk opened his own mail.
Zachary Taylor strode these halls like a god.
Nothing much occurred to Rutherford B. Hayes.
Franklin Delano Roosevelt invented aspirin.
Chester Arthur borrowed more sugar than his neighbor.
Harry S. Truman walked with a limp,
which alarmed the usually placid John Adams.
Ulysses S. Grant liked to knit during idle moments.
The saga of James Garfield began in Nova Scotia.
Richard Nixon would do anything for a milkshake.

NORTH OZYMANDIAN

Above the wind
there's nothing
but wind—
a shred
not meant
to be shared
shared.
What was inside
now spans.
Wind allows
no opposite
or obverse.
There's
just wind.

///

A watery horizon
between you.
There is
no distance
to discuss.
No sand
to sift.
Only stone.

///

You're far
into the fog.
It lines
every side
of you.
Your skin
thick with it.
Sudden sun.

MY HERON

The heron, of course, is not mine
though I think of it as "my heron"
when I find it at the pond,
the artificial pond that has "Lake"
in its name, the pond that is drained
every June so the keepers of the grounds
can clean whatever needs to be cleaned
beneath the impenetrable brown surface:
bottles and cans, condoms and cans,
whatever collects, even books,
and once, a chair, as if waiting there
for someone to claim and then occupy
the space it proffered.
There are ducks, and geese,
aggressive if you appear with bread
or carry something of your own to eat.
There are turtles, at least four.
The largest tends to linger
by the rocks while his smaller kin
venture farther. But only
the heron, my heron,
owns the whole scene.
He occupies the shore,
and when he chooses, lifts and soars
above, then across, the pond,
to reoccupy the shore.

He is not concerned with the depths
except as another thing to cross,
gives them neither first nor second glance.
I chart my own position by the heron,
can feel the pond turn to muck
when he is not within sight.
I do not know where he goes
when the pond turns to ice.

MOUNTAIN TOWN

All the feet
confused.

MOSTLY SUNNY

A blue day
spoiled by one
asshole cloud.

MINERVAL MORNING

Head split
as if
in two.

MESCAL'S WAGER

Down
in case of
absence.

LISTENING TOUR

There is no
bird here
going peep.

LIKE GRASS

Fall too late
to plant. Ground
cover. Clover.

LICE HUNTERS

after Rimbaud

The boy's sisters,
their sharp fingers.

GRAND DESIGN

We know
there is no grand design,
no figure
from which we emerged
already buried,
or unburied
as if born,
no field
where everyone
is welcomed
(to play) (to bring
their ball of words,
their bag of myths).
There is no order, no
form
holding it all
together,
no one
to hold any
thing together.
But there is this
(there is this):
you, me,
this collage
of particulars
larger, somehow,

than the known universe,
which, we've heard,
is expanding.

GLASS CORONA

As if the sky reflected there
possessed nothing but its carbony face
and the sporadic soliton or flare,

as if its cap were actually a base,
upstep rather than endpoint,
the shadow a sudden vertical trace

astonishing the glass, a taunt
cutting off the view of above,
a sliver of that view, a phant

-om before the eye, a glove
across the face (once, twice),
but here no pretense of love

appears as if to entice
the eye into the window
—no, through the window, slice

by colloidal slice, row after row
of sight portioned into strips,
wounds only the eye can know

and, knowing, own, sight's eclipse
a consequence of searching for sky
in glass when glass is apocalypse,

scraps and specks, sand and dust blown awry,
easily broken and easily mistaken,
a trick so evident it fools not the eye

but the brain behind it, unshaken
and buried inside the skull, a filigreed
reminder of what the face has forsaken

every time it's the eye's turn to feed,
to gorge on, scan, or measure what,
in glass, cannot be reflected.

2.

Even if the eye were half shut,
the sky would hang itself, rope or no,
in whatever light was portioned out

for the watcher, always poised below
what she also stands inside, asking
Where does the sky begin, a slow

bleed above the trees masking
the horizon, that sad marker
stuck between feeding and fasting,

swollen between dark and darker,
the branches scratching the surface
of the sky, which stretches no farther

than itself, downward, reflects
what the unadorned eye
can see and, seeing, confess

what it seeks and, seeking, defy,
not the image within the reflection
but the image on the other side,

the sky not window but mirror
without the silver lining its back,
a breathing sheen of sorrowed glass

that flashes and swells from lack to lack
and, swollen, pushes to shatter
the shards that fall from every crack,

descend this wavering ladder
and explode in pools of broken light,
the image awash in prism's scatter,

that is where the sky begins, where night
collides with darkness and a temperature
that has buried what was once called sight.

3.

The opening (read: aperture)
is open by design (read: default),
so susceptible to departure

with the brain floating, bag of salt,
loud, malleable light, the sky profuse
in its movement from rim to vault,

an orb (read: void) open to obtuse
approach from any outer corridor
(read: vector), as if angle could produce

what sight announces as visitor,
a gravity-infected flash, or fleck,
that, focused, becomes meteor,

the surface less limit than wreck,
the eye a crash site, open to air,
onto a sky that will not reflect.

GHOST FONT

Reset with what
was erased and,
erased, retained.

FOUND PORTRAIT

I met you on the sidewalk
I met you near the record store
I grabbed a Slurpee and sucked it down
I followed a whim and see where it got me
I asked a question of every squirrel I saw
I heaved and I suffered and I heaved no more
I wandered and got lost in the mall
I looked you in the eye as I shook your hand
I watched you split the ounce in three
1/3 for you 1/3 for him 1/3 for me
I eavesdropped on his death threat
I wished the door was locked
I clipped all the coupons
I was evicted before I'd unpacked the car
I was stranded when my axle broke
I caught the cat by its collar
I can barely see the scars
I borrowed a book only to write in it
I asked the urinal what it thought
I inked those words on the wall
My spirit broke before my back
I raced before I walked
I never mind over matter
I climbed down after climbing up

FORMER PLANET

Percolates
in the shape
of a pill.

FORGOTTEN FORM

lost
in its
finding

FOR RENT

we sell
our days.

FOOD COURT

An hour burnished
as if time could bear
a sheen.

FLOTATION DEVICE

Begs
the
question.

FIRST FACE

in a new light
we forget
is a dead light.

FIELD GUIDE

To be
so inclined.

EYE OUT

I am my own
civil war
is what I wrote
in my sleep,
in the sleep
where a plane
descending
grazed
with a wing
a tree
in a park
in Dallas.
There was no runway
until I saw it,
a dirt road
at the park's edge.
A headline
in the cabin
declared The Age
of Empathy.
I tried to follow
the seams.
Other things
happened
on that plane
but let's not dwell
on a dream.

EXEMPLARY LIFE

I hate
the original

ELEGY, PREMATURE
for Tomaž

It's said you were the bird
at your own funeral.
At least you didn't miss it,
like my other father, lost
luggage, late for his own burial.
Departure, arrival.
At least you didn't swell
like him, three days bloat
in his 1BR apartment.

Now I read the you you left behind,
the words, and carry some across.
There's no way to unsee
the world without you.
No way to unhear your voice,
to recognize this changed air.
I may have forgotten
what an elegy is
but I know this:
you have not left. Not yet.
Not every winged creature
needs a nest.

ELECTORAL COLLEGE

You lose whatever you find
and are left with loss
which becomes its own thing
heavy at times
at times almost imperceptible
as if your brain had managed
to sever that connection
fill in the rut that makes you
hold on when what you want
is to strip the mind bare
of dead connections

EAST AIR

What liquid's
distilled
inside

a cloud
that hangs
on(to itself)

for (one more
hour of)
dear life

///

How does
the noise
outside oneself

so easily
drown out
the noise within

///

Every thought
revisited
makes the ditch

through which it travels
that much wider
harder to fill

EARTH'S MUSTACHE

There is, of course, Theodore
Roosevelt National Park.
You must have forgotten that
beacon of Bismarck, ND.
And now you're telling me Plains
is not on your radar (o
kay, "not in [your] repertoire").

You still consider Pluto
a full-fledged planet, a red
planet hot, the Sun a ball
of gas. You forgot one need
not be assassinated
to die in office. One need
not die to die in office.

Whitehorse is colorless.
Wilderness is not wildness.
Three is no longer the prime
number of choice. It's seven:
colors in the visible
spectrum, days of the week, con
tinents flitting the planet.

Landscape is all about con
trast (fuck deserts, fuck grasslands).
Park the visual splendor.
Capture the individual
looming (fuck swamp, fuck prairies).
Elevate the kernel. Plus
the core. That helium core.

Who thought the sun had a moon,
was it you? The sun is no
Saturn. Even Eris has one.
To spend all day spinning round.
As if your terms must be con
secutive. As if boron
were born to stretch, or harden.

As if colors could contain
what they name. As if phosphor
us weren't the nastiest stuff.
White, not black. And Nunavut?
Left out in the cold again.
Andrew Johnson's polar bear
garden its closest neighbor.

Every planet has two poles.
Hydrogen suffers regard
less of surface. The Arctic,
where is it? Franz Josef Land
just sits there, excluded from
the eleven time zones, click
clacking over the expanse.

DISASTER RELIEF

DESIGN FLAW

How it glares,
awash in in
-significance.

DEFINE REJECTION

As one gives way to another
so does the asphalt interrupt
what was bound to emerge
as the crux of the event.

We do not bow our heads
or mutter into our drinks,
but embrace the failure with which
others have garnished us.

We soak in it like we soak
in our pissed-in Levi's.
We suck it down and throw it down
and roll it up for later, to savor.

No sad sacks here.
No pity parties or elephant nuts.
We welcome what's been heaped on us.
Thank you very much.

DEAR DECOMPOSER

When touched

the dog-vomit fungus
dappled across the mulch

poofs into the air
but is otherwise 'harmless'

unlike artillery fungus
which shoots itself

up to fifteen feet up
onto the house

and will not come off
or down

and is attracted by light
and which none of us has seen

DAY CARE

Insert
child
here.

CAREFUL NOW

That's a baby
you're holding.

BLANK PAGE

Loud
white
space.

BIRD EXPLOSION

Open window
wet with
speed.

BACKGROUND NOISE

Sad
little
scratches.

AFTER WINTER

No way of knowing when this sick began.
A string that stretches beyond the dirt horizon.

A wasp and a hawk drift and glide. Pollen
has fallen on all the surfaces, and now the wasp,

slapped from air to ground where it will shell
and husk until the next hard rain erases it.

The wet string expands. The sick horizon rivers.
There is no dirt anywhere. Nothing hangs in the air.

///

Which bone protrudes first when a body is broken?

Which limb cries out to the brain to save it?
What is left of the skin removed from the limb?

The mud swallows all the surfaces. The rain shrieks.
The air allows nothing but sound to ride it.

Mud so thick the string fails the horizon,
falls to the ground to be embraced by mud.

///

The sick, the mud, the rain suck the air from the air.
There is no breathing here. Throats only rattle

in a constant attempt to clear. The sputter fills the air.
Phlegm and wet, wet. The mud inches in.

The pollen swallowed, every shell and limb.
Mud annuls the skin horizon, sucks and pulls.

The rain stops. The flood stretches, climbs.
Nothing moves in the mud. Nothing thinks to move.

///

We slide down from the trees we had climbed
and walk across the mud bored hard by the sun,

gather to measure what this thicker earth
has given us: a surface above where our heads had been,

a soft horizon open to any who approach it,
a fresh desert marked only by the tops of trees.

The sky has grown closer. The new surface lifts us
toward the stars, the thread that holds us down.

///

And we know the rain will not fall again,
the dirt never turn to mud beneath us.

We know the sky will shrink until what lies beyond
closes in and we can ascend. The thinner sky within reach

and pulsing so hard we cannot hear the breath
that builds inside the mud, a gasp at first, then cough.

And we know the earth is full now, too full and dead to flood.

///

The stars have been wiped from the sky.

Only the fragment of moon,
a chipped, stray tooth

one bite away from falling out
of its dying mouth, hangs there.

An apology. An alibi. All of creation
a crime scene. Everything alive a victim.

We follow the tooth until morning then climb
into the crania of trees to sleep. A loose sleep.

AFTER AFTER

Black streaks slather the sun. The sky's tooth
has come undone, floats dirtward, away from us.

We follow it, night's lacquer, until the sun bursts
over the horizon so fast half of us char

before we find trees to block it.

///

The heavy horizon pulls the earth faster,
the sun gone in an hour. Now the toothless night.

We find the moon later that night. More pink
than white, it is soft in our hands—wet sand.

We tear it apart, tear the already broken moon
into pieces. For our mouths. For our pockets and hollows.

One of us (was it you?) discovers that wringing
the moon, like a neck, yields liquid. We quench.

///

The sun struggles at the edge all day, a day all dawn,
but cannot lift itself into the sky. No rise or noon,

no dusk. Finally the horizon frees itself
and the sun falls back out of sight.

We eat what's left of the half-dead and dying trees,
walk in the dark and sleep on the ground in the dark.

///

With nothing to eat, we walk. With nothing else to find.

We decide to remain on the blackdark dirt
under the blackdark hole-strewn sky.

With nothing to watch, we wait. There is nowhere
to go, nowhere worth going.

We sleep, and as we sleep the horizon swells
on every side. What's left shrinks.

///

We measure the remaining space by sleeps.
The edge is now four sleeps away, now three.

Two. Even the sky is squeezed, the once-scattered holes
grow closer, then together. A new moon.

One of us (was it all of us?) tries to reach it, to climb
through and out. But it is too far and we are too tired.

The horizon collapses on us
as we start to fall asleep. Into sleep.

AERIAL CAMPAIGN

Because the river offers a vista
Because the fires enliven the horizon
Because the park is a labyrinth
sometimes a fortress
Because the crane has become the edifice
Because the lights at the window
Because *space is only time visible*
Because one river swallows another
Because the city like a city
The dog stiff in the flowerbed
Because *voices of the dead*
they are not dead
who hears them?
Because water is water
and always moving
Because sleep is a gift
with no giver

1000 FLIGHTS

One lame continent.
The sun fails. The fences
rise up.